T0043229

Where Is the White House?

by Megan Stine

illustrated by David Groff

Penguin Workshop

For Bill and Cody—MS

For Alana, Elise, and Grant—DG

PENGUIN WORKSHOP
An Imprint of Penguin Random House LLC, New York

Text copyright © 2015 by Megan Stine.
Illustrations copyright © 2015 by Penguin Random House LLC. All rights reserved.
Published by Penguin Workshop, an imprint of Penguin Random House LLC, New York.
PENGUIN and PENGUIN WORKSHOP are trademarks of Penguin Books Ltd.
WHO HQ & Design is a registered trademark of Penguin Random House LLC.
Printed in the USA.

Visit us online at www.penguinrandomhouse.com.

Library of Congress Control Number: 2014044375

ISBN 9780448483559   20 19 18 17 16 15 14

Contents

Where Is the White House?

On a fall day in 1792, President George Washington stood in a muddy pit on a barren rise of land. Rolling hills nearby were surrounded by woods. Cows and pigs grazed in the distance. No one lived anywhere near this beautiful wilderness overlooking the Potomac River.

Washington picked up a hammer and drove a stake into the ground. Then he drove another. And another. Those stakes told the workmen exactly where to put the corners and walls of a new house. George Washington was the first president of the United States. But he was also a surveyor—a person who measures land.

A whole new city was going to be built! It would be the capital city for the new country of the United States of America. The house at the center of it would be the new President's House.

It would take eight years, many laborers, and tons of stone before the house was complete. George Washington never even got to live there. But eventually, the White House stood exactly where the first president said it should go, and the new capital city was named for him—the city of Washington.

CHAPTER 1
Building a Capital City

It was 1783. The Revolutionary War was over. The colonists had fought against the British for eight long years to gain their freedom. Finally, the colonists had won! A new country was born— the United States of America.

Now it was time to go about the business of creating a government. Like any other country, America would need a capital city. The city would need to have buildings for the government to work in. And it would need an important house for the president to live in.

Where should that capital city be?

At that time, some people thought the capital should be in Philadelphia, Pennsylvania. After all, that's where the first Congress met. It's also where the Founding Fathers signed the Declaration of Independence.

But one day something scary happened. A mob of angry men stormed up to the building where Congress was meeting. Congress asked Pennsylvania to protect them from the mob. The governor of Pennsylvania refused to help. He thought the angry men were in the right!

That made the men in Congress think twice about where the capital should be. They decided it should not be in any of the thirteen states. It should be separate, on a special piece of land. Then the US government could have soldiers to protect and defend the capital city, without ever asking any state for help.

In 1790, Congress decided that the new capital city would be built along the Potomac River.

MASS

NH

MASS

NY

RI

CONN

NJ

PA

MD

DEL

ATLANTIC
OCEAN

VA

POTOMAC
RIVER

NC

SC

GA

The spot they chose was part of Maryland and Virginia. Congress picked the spot to please the southern states. In exchange for having the capital in the south, the southern states agreed that the whole country should pay some debts from the war for the northern states. Now everyone was happy. Both Maryland and Virginia agreed to give up the land for the new city.

President George Washington hired a French architect named Pierre L'Enfant to design the city. L'Enfant had big ideas. He designed the entire city of Washington, DC, on a grand scale. The main avenues in the new capital would be wide. They would lead into huge traffic circles. There would also be long diagonal streets. Important statues and monuments would be lined up with one another. That way people could stand at one important building and look straight down the avenue to another one.

L'Enfant planned that the President's House would sit at one end of a big diagonal street. The Capitol building, where Congress would meet, would sit at the other end. Straight across from the President's House, he thought there should be a statue of George Washington riding on a horse.

L'Enfant drew up the plans and gave them to George Washington. Washington liked the plans, but not everyone agreed about the house. L'Enfant had set aside more than eighty acres of land for a "Presidential Palace." Thomas Jefferson, one of the Founding Fathers, thought a big house was a bad

Thomas Jefferson

idea. He said it would be too grand and showy. It would seem like Washington was trying to be a king—not a president elected to serve the people.

Jefferson said they should hold a contest to see who could come up with a design for the house. Washington agreed. So the contest was announced, and several people sent in designs. Some of the drawings looked like palaces or churches. One of them even had a throne inside. And one design was sent in anonymously—without a name on it. It was probably sent in by Thomas Jefferson! He very much wanted to help design the President's House.

George Washington had his own ideas, though. He had already met a builder he liked. His name was James Hoban. Washington invited Hoban to enter the contest. He met with Hoban privately. They probably talked about what kind of house Washington wanted. And guess what? Hoban won the contest!

There was only one thing Washington didn't like about Hoban's design. It was too small! It was five times smaller than the palace L'Enfant had planned. So George Washington told the builders to make the house one-fifth bigger. He also told the workmen

James Hoban

to add a lot of carvings of leaves and flowers around the front door, to make it fancier.

Many of the workmen on the new house were slaves who had been "rented" from their owners. They had to work for free. They were good, strong laborers, but they weren't trained to do carvings in stone. So workers were brought to America from Scotland to create the beautiful carvings on the front of the new house. Free African Americans also worked to build the house.

Slavery and the White House

For more than two hundred years, slavery was allowed in America. Twelve of our presidents owned slaves, eight of them while in office. George Washington owned more than two hundred.

Sometimes they worked in the White House as servants—right beside white servants who were being paid.

President James K. Polk's wife, Sarah, wanted to save money, so she fired the paid white servants—and brought in slaves instead.

The most famous enslaved person to live in the White House was Paul Jennings. He came to the White House at the age of ten, with President James Madison. Paul helped Dolley Madison when the White House was set on fire. He remained a slave and a servant for many years. After James Madison died, Paul was freed. He wrote the first book about life in the White House.

In 1865, Congress finally passed a law that ended slavery once and for all.

Paul
Jennings

The house Hoban designed would become the White House—although it wouldn't be called that for many years. When it was being built, it wasn't even white! It was made from light brown sandstone—a kind of stone that has many tiny holes in it. If rain got in and then the water froze, the stones could crack. So the President's House was immediately painted with whitewash to fill the holes.

George Washington died in 1799, a year before the house was completed. The father of our country is the only president who never got the chance to live in the White House.

Was James Hoban a Copycat?

James Hoban, the architect who designed the White House, was born in Ireland. He went to school in Dublin, the capital of Ireland. The biggest, most important house in Dublin at that time was called Leinster House. It was the home of the Duke of Leinster—a famous and powerful man.

George Washington admired the Duke of Leinster. So George Washington probably wanted the President's House to be as grand as the most famous house in Dublin.

We don't know for sure whether Hoban meant to copy Leinster House. But the White House and Leinster House look very much alike. Both buildings have four columns in front. The columns support a triangular shape—called a pediment—over the door. Both have tall rows of windows across, with fancy pediments above them.

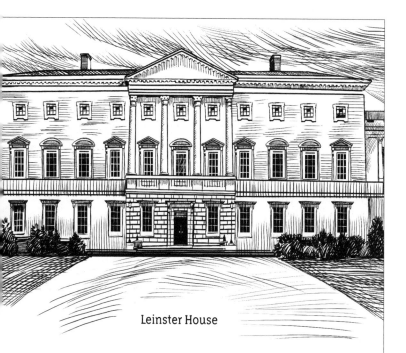

Leinster House

Hoban built several other buildings in America. They look a lot like Leinster House, too! Was he a copycat? Or was he just doing what so many artists do—learning from the masters of the past?

CHAPTER 2
Fire!

John Adams, the second president, moved into the White House in November 1800. His wife, Abigail, was supposed to join him two weeks later. But she could barely find the house! The new roads leading into the city weren't marked.

It was still a wilderness. They made a wrong turn and got lost. In fact, the woods surrounding the new capital were so thick, Abigail's carriage couldn't get through! The coachman had to chop off branches from the trees as they rode along.

Abigail finally got to the White House, but she didn't live there for long. Her husband, John Adams, was not elected for a second term. He and Abigail had to move out just a few months after they moved in.

Abigail didn't mind leaving. The White House was bitterly cold inside. Why? There were plenty of trees for firewood—but no one around to chop it! Very few people lived there. It was hard to find workers. And the Adamses didn't believe in using slave labor.

Life was hard for Abigail. She and her husband had only brought a few servants with them. She had to hang her own washing up to dry on clotheslines in the huge East Room in the White House!

The next president was Thomas Jefferson. Jefferson had secretly wanted to design the White House. Now he was finally living in it and making changes he wanted. Right away, he hired workmen to finish the rooms inside.

He also added two wings to the house—one on the east side and one on the west. These long, low wings had rooms for all the practical work that needed to be done. There was a laundry, a dairy, a smokehouse for preparing meat, a stable, and more.

Jefferson also changed the landscape. He planted trees and drew up plans for flower and vegetable gardens. He had a stone wall built around

the grounds, but it didn't keep people out. For several years, there was an open market right in front of the White House. People even held horse races in the front yard!

After eight years as president, Jefferson left the White House, in 1809. By then, the city of Washington was beginning to grow. More houses were built. The long diagonal streets had names—

they were named for states. Pennsylvania Avenue ran right past the President's House.

The next president, James Madison, and his wife, Dolley, were famous for giving parties. At one huge party, Dolley Madison served a fancy new dessert that few Americans had eaten—strawberry ice cream! Sometimes, she even served ice cream wrapped in hot pastry. She also took charge of decorating the White House. The First Lady, as the wife of the president came to be called, added drapes, mirrors, nice furniture, and elegant lighting fixtures.

But her furnishings did not last long. In 1812, America and England were at war again. Two years later, the British marched into Washington, DC.

They came to take over the capital city and burn the White House!

Dolley Madison knew the British soldiers were coming. Word had arrived that a hundred soldiers were marching toward the house. The president was away with the troops. What should she do?

Dolley Madison knew she had to leave. But first she had the servants take down the huge portrait of George Washington that hung on the wall. She and the servants tried to save other precious things as well. Then they all fled to safety. Just in time!

When the British soldiers arrived, they found a delicious meal waiting for them. It was the dinner the servants had cooked for the president! The soldiers sat down, ate the meal, and drank all the special wine.

Then they set the White House on fire!

The house burned for hours, well into the night, until a hard rain began to fall. People stood and watched the blaze in shock. The President's House was so grand and so new! It was only fourteen years old.

When the fire was over, the entire inside of the White House had been destroyed. Most of the walls were weakened, too. A few walls were standing, but almost the whole building had to be rebuilt, from the ground up.

It took three years to restore the White House. Many of the burned and scorched stones—especially the beautifully carved pieces—were reused. To cover up the black scorch marks, the house was painted white. From then on, the nickname "White House" was used more and more. In 1901, President Theodore Roosevelt made it the official name.

CHAPTER 3
Constant Change

After the fire, the White House was rebuilt pretty much as it had been before. But was it finished? No way.

In the 1820s, porticos—tall covered entrances with columns—were added to the north and south entrances of the building. The porticos made the White House look even more important and impressive when people arrived.

After that, every president made changes of one sort or another. But the house was not always treated with respect. President Andrew Jackson had a huge party when he was elected in 1829. He invited the public to come. Mobs of people swarmed into the White House. They stood on

chairs with their muddy boots and pushed and shoved to get a look at the president. Thousands of dollars' worth of china were broken. The White House was a mess! Andrew Jackson had to climb out a window to escape the mob. The only way to get people to leave the house was to set up tubs of alcohol on the lawn!

In 1861 President Abraham Lincoln, with his wife and sons, moved in. The Lincolns found the White House rooms had become shabby. So Congress gave the president twenty thousand dollars to redecorate. It was a huge amount of money in those days. But First Lady Mary Todd Lincoln spent even more! She bought very expensive curtains and a carved mahogany bed.

The country was now embroiled in a Civil War, so her spending seemed wrong. Why should she buy fancy furniture when soldiers didn't even have blankets? It made the public—and her husband—very angry. In fact, President Lincoln was so mad at her, he probably never slept in the bed! Today, it's called the Lincoln Bed, but President Lincoln probably never slept there.

Even though Mrs. Lincoln spent more than she should have, Congress still gives each new president money to decorate the White House.

Electric Lights

There was no electric lighting in the White House until 1891. Benjamin Harrison was president at the time. Before that, the only lights in the White House came from candles or gas lamps. At first, no one thought electric lights would be reliable. They thought it was just a backup for the gas lights!

President Harrison and his wife refused to touch the light switches. They were afraid they'd get a shock! So they made the servants turn all the lights on and off.

In 1902, President Teddy Roosevelt decided to redo the White House completely. Roosevelt had a good reason to make changes. He and his wife had six children! The children needed room to play, and the president needed a quieter place to work. So Teddy added an office building onto the west wing of the White House. But senators and congressmen refused to meet him there. They thought the new West Wing wasn't an important enough place. They only wanted to meet the president in the White House itself.

In 1933 another Roosevelt became president. Franklin Delano Roosevelt, a distant cousin of Teddy Roosevelt, was known as FDR. He decided to make the West Wing even bigger. He wanted offices for all of his staff—and he wanted them nearby. A disease called polio had left FDR unable to walk, so he had a ramp built. His chair could roll right into the West Wing without going up any steps. He also had a swimming pool installed indoors. Swimming was the best exercise for a man with his condition. Schoolchildren sent in money to help pay for the pool!

After FDR died in 1945, Vice President Harry Truman became president. One day, a leg from his daughter's grand piano crashed through the floor! Truman realized that the White House had fallen into terrible disrepair. The wooden beams used after the fire of 1814 weren't strong enough to support all the weight in the house. Adding plumbing and electricity over the years had also weakened the floors. It was dangerous to live there.

So from 1948 till 1952, Harry and Bess Truman and their daughter, Margaret, moved out of the White House—and the whole house was gutted! New basements were dug out with bulldozers. Then the whole house was rebuilt using steel beams, plaster, and solid stone. Most of the rooms were rebuilt in the same shapes and sizes as they had been before. Old doors, chandeliers, and fireplace mantels were saved and reused. Fancy plaster designs from the ceilings were copied in the new rooms. When it was done, the White House was completely new inside, but it looked historic.

Truman changed a few things, though. He changed the Grand Staircase. He also added a balcony over the South Portico. Today, it's called the Truman Balcony. Presidents and their families love to sit out there. It's like having a private porch looking out over the backyard.

The most recent person to make important

changes to the White House was Jacqueline Kennedy. As First Lady, she redecorated the whole house in 1961. She added valuable antiques and made the main floor of the house look like a museum. Famous paintings were hung on the walls. Jackie Kennedy said that the White House wasn't just a house for the president's family. It was also a national treasure.

From then on, presidents were allowed to redecorate their private rooms on the second floor of the White House. But they couldn't change the Ground or State Floors without getting the okay from a historical committee.

When Jackie Kennedy was finished redecorating, she gave a tour of the White House—on TV! Millions of people watched. To viewers, it felt like everyone in America had been invited inside the most glamorous house in the world.

CHAPTER 4
Take a Tour

Welcome to the White House!

As you walk in through the front door—wait a minute. Where is the front door, anyway?

The north side of the White House is the official "front door" of 1600 Pennsylvania Avenue. (That's the White House's address.) For many years, people used to be able to walk right in through the North Portico. There was no gate around the house—and no guards! There was a public park in front. People felt free to come and go as they liked. At one time, there were even cows on the front lawn. And sheep. (President Woodrow Wilson let a flock of sheep graze there during World War I, so the government wouldn't have to pay to mow the lawn. And he auctioned off the wool to raise money for the Red Cross.)

Today, the White House is surrounded by a tall iron fence. No one uses the front door, or North Portico, to enter anymore, except on very special occasions. When a queen or king or other important leader comes to dinner, they will enter through the North Portico.

After a new president takes office, the First Family arrives through that same door. Otherwise, most people enter the White House from the side or back—and only after going through several different security-guard checkpoints!

Inside the White House there are six floors, including the basements.

The main floor is called the State Floor. It includes the rooms where nearly all the public events are held. The president and his family sleep upstairs on the second floor, but that wasn't always the case. In the past, some families slept on the first floor and had offices upstairs.

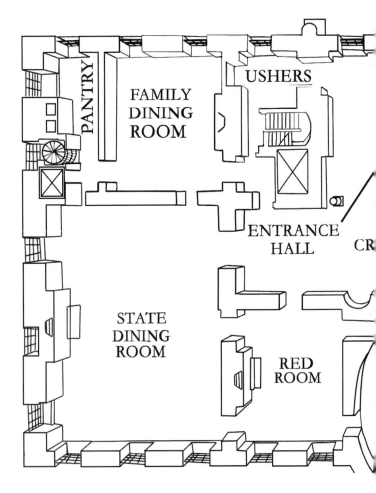

The biggest room in the White House is called the East Room. At eighty feet long and thirty-seven feet wide, it's almost the size of a high-school basketball court! Today, the East Room is used for parties, concerts, dinners, and press conferences.

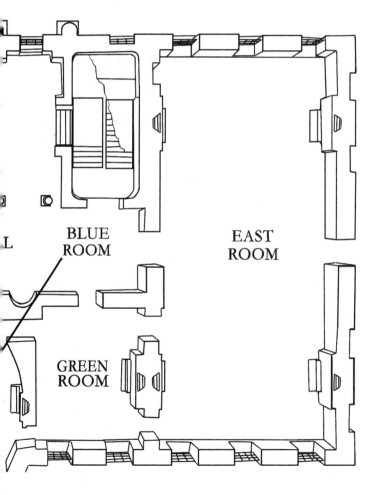

BLUE
ROOM

EAST
ROOM

GREEN
ROOM

Several presidents' daughters have gotten married in the East Room. And President Ford's daughter Susan had her high-school prom there in 1975!

When George Washington helped design the White House, he had other plans for the East Room. He wanted this big room to be a place where Congress would come to present laws for the president to sign. That didn't happen much at first. But President Lyndon B. Johnson signed an important law in the East Room—the Civil Rights Act of 1964. He had to use the biggest room in the White House because so many people wanted to watch him sign it!

After President Lincoln was shot in April 1865, his body was brought to the East Room to lie in state. That meant people could walk past and pay their respects to the dead president. For the funeral, the chandeliers and mirrors were covered with black silk.

Thomas Jefferson thought the East Room was too grand and fancy. So he let his secretary, a man named Meriwether Lewis, live there. Teddy Roosevelt used to hold boxing matches in the East Room. He would set up a boxing ring and invite people to fight him. In one match, a young soldier punched Roosevelt and accidentally blinded him in his left eye.

On the opposite side of the house is another large room called the State Dining Room. This is where huge state dinners are held—dinners for the head of a foreign country. On those occasions, the president makes a toast to the guest of honor. For just that moment, the press is allowed to come in.

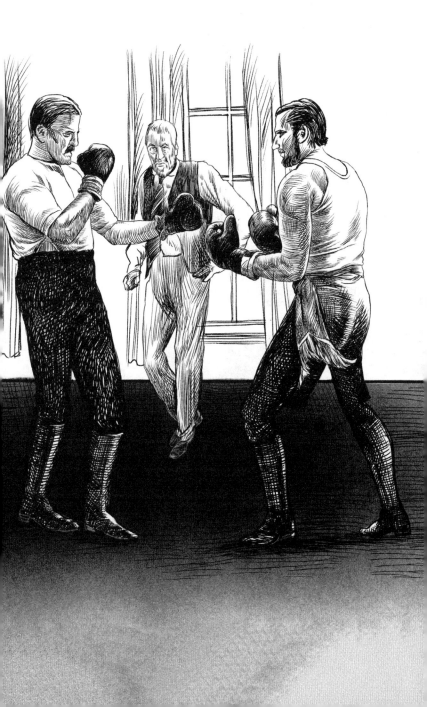

All of a sudden, special hidden compartments in the columns swing open—and TV lighting swings out! With the lights blazing, the TV cameramen photograph the president's speech. Then the lights are put away and the press must leave.

In between the two largest rooms, there are three very beautiful smaller rooms on the State Floor. They are named for the colors used on the walls and furnishings—the Green Room, the Blue Room, and the Red Room.

The most important of the three is right in the middle of the White House—the Blue Room. It should really be called the Oval Room because that's what shape it is. If you look at the White House from the back, you'll see that the building has a curved bulge in the middle. That's where the oval Blue Room is located. There's also a Yellow Oval Room upstairs, right above it.

The Blue Room is an oval because George Washington wanted a special place for people to come meet the president. In the early days, the president would have a weekly event called a levee. During the levee, all the guests stood in a circle. The president would greet them as he walked around the circle and bowed to each one. Since the levee was held in a circle, Washington thought it should happen in a round or oval room.

The Blue Room was also used to welcome visitors when the White House was open to the public on New Year's Day, which used to be a tradition.

On January 1, 1863, President Lincoln stood in the Blue Room for hours, shaking hands with the public. Then he went upstairs and signed one of the most important documents in American history—the Emancipation Proclamation. It freed all the slaves in the southern states at war with the north.

Right next to the Blue Room, on the left, is the Green Room. Today, it's one of the most beautiful and cozy spots in the White House. Used as a parlor or sitting room, the Green Room is filled with paintings, sofas, chairs, and a fireplace. But in years past, it may have been used as a bedroom by John Adams's secretary. It was used as a dining room by Thomas Jefferson. And when Mary and Abraham Lincoln's young son Willie died, his body was embalmed in the Green Room.

To the right of the oval Blue Room is the Red Room. Abraham Lincoln loved to sit by the fire in the Red Room and read newspapers. Richard Nixon had his family's Thanksgiving dinner there in 1970.

The second floor of the White House is private. That's where the president and the First Family relax. Their bedrooms, living room, family kitchen, and guest rooms are there.

There are also several fancy, formal rooms upstairs. Those are used as guest rooms for important visitors. A rose-colored bedroom is called the Queens' Bedroom because seven queens have slept there!

One of the most famous rooms in the White House is called the Lincoln Bedroom, even though he never slept there. He used it as an office when he was president. Today, only close friends or important guests are invited to sleep in the Lincoln Bedroom. It's considered a huge treat.

But some people think that a nice hotel would be more comfortable. People say the Lincoln Bed is lumpy!

Altogether, there are 132 rooms in the White House. There are thirty-five bathrooms now, but there weren't always so many. In fact, the first presidents had to go outside to an outhouse to use the toilet! Thomas Jefferson installed two toilets indoors, but not everyone could use them. The servants had to use the outhouse.

President Franklin Pierce added the first bathtub to the White House in 1853. He had hot water brought into the house, too. But a normal size tub wasn't big enough for William Taft, who was president from 1909 to 1913. He weighed more than three hundred pounds! Taft had to have a giant tub made especially for him.

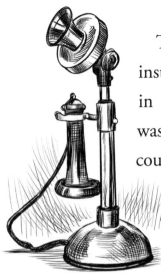

The first telephone was installed in the White House in 1879. The phone number was "1"! At the time, the phone could only call one other place— the Treasury Department.

Today, the White House has twenty-eight fireplaces, three elevators, a movie theater, and a bowling alley. On the Ground Floor, there's a flower shop, a doctor's office, and even a chocolate shop. On the top

floor there's a pool table, a music room, a workout room, a rooftop deck, a sunroom, and several more bedrooms. Plenty of room for sleepovers! One thing is for sure: People living in the White House will never get bored!

CHAPTER 5
The West Wing

If you stand on Pennsylvania Avenue, smack in front of the White House, you can barely see the West Wing. The ground slopes down a bit beside the big house, so both wings of the White House are hidden.

The West Wing

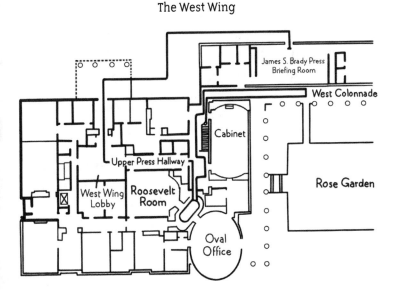

But the West Wing is every bit as important as the White House itself, because that's where the president's office is. The president's office is called the Oval Office. It was designed as an oval to match the oval Blue Room in the White House. When a president speaks to the American public on TV about a big decision, the speech will often be broadcast from the Oval Office.

The West Wing is so important that a popular show called *The West Wing* was on TV for many years. It showed what it's like to work in the busiest part of the White House.

The West Wing was originally built by Teddy Roosevelt. Then President Taft made it bigger. But on Christmas Eve in 1929, while Herbert Hoover was president, there was a terrible fire. It was so cold out that the water in the firemen's hoses froze! The West Wing was gutted.

FDR rebuilt the West Wing and made it even bigger. He had the Oval Office moved to the corner. From there, the president can look out to the West Colonnade—the long walkway with columns that connects the West Wing to the White House. The president's office also faces the pretty Rose Garden.

The Oval Office has four doors in it. Two of the doors are sort of secret doors. They blend into the wall, so you don't notice them. One of the secret doors leads to the office of the president's secretary; it has a peephole, so the president's secretary can peek in. That way, the secretary knows whether it's okay to interrupt the president. The other secret door goes into the main hallway. The third door leads to the president's private dining room. The fourth door leads outside to the Rose Garden.

Each president is allowed to redecorate the Oval Office. They get a new oval rug, new drapes, new wallpaper, new furniture, and new artwork for the walls.

The president can also choose which desk to use. Many presidents have chosen a famous desk called the Resolute desk. The desk was made from wooden beams taken from a British ship called the *Resolute*.

The ship got trapped in the ice north of Canada in 1854. When Americans found the ship in 1855, they sent it back to England.

Queen Victoria was so grateful, she decided to have a desk made from the wood. She gave the desk to President Hayes as a thank-you gift in 1880.

When FDR used the Resolute, he didn't want people to see his legs in his wheelchair. He added a panel at the front to cover the opening.

The Resolute desk became even more famous when John F. Kennedy used it. His two-year-old son, John, sometimes hid underneath. He liked to swing open the panel door. Surprise!

Some presidents spend a lot of time in the Oval Office. Some don't. In the mid-1960s, President Lyndon B. Johnson had a whole row

of televisions set up there, so he could watch the news on every channel at once!

What else happens in the West Wing? The Cabinet Room is next to the Oval Office. This is where the president holds his Cabinet meetings—meetings with all the important people on his team.

Inside the Cabinet Room there's a long table with a chair for each member. The president's chair is a few inches taller than everyone else's—of course!

What Is the Cabinet?

The Cabinet is the name of the group of people who are appointed by the president to help run the government. Each Cabinet member runs a different department. For example, the head of the Department of Education is called the Secretary of Education. In this case, "secretary" doesn't mean someone who takes notes or writes letters for the boss. It means the person who is in charge!

Other Cabinet members include the Secretary of State, the Secretary of the Treasury, and more. Altogether, not counting the president and vice president, there are currently twenty-two members of the Cabinet—more than ever. The Cabinet is getting to be so big, the people barely fit around the table.

Each Cabinet member has his or her own chair in the Cabinet Room. Their names are on the chairs.

When they leave the job, their special chair is given to them as a gift. Some people have been part of the president's Cabinet many times. They get to take home three or four different chairs!

Another famous room in the West Wing is called the Roosevelt Room. It's right across the hall from the Oval Office. It wasn't always called the Roosevelt Room, though. It used to be called the Fish Room! FDR kept fish tanks in there, and put his fishing trophies on the wall.

None of the presidents who came after FDR liked calling it the Fish Room, so President Nixon decided to rename it. He called it the Roosevelt Room after the two presidents who built the West Wing.

On the Ground Floor of the West Wing, there's a special restaurant and dining room called the White House Mess. Why? Not because it's messy! It's called the Mess because the navy runs it—and in the navy, a dining room is called a mess hall. The White House Mess is a very fancy room, with wood paneling on the walls and white linen tablecloths. Only high-level people are allowed to eat there. The White House Mess also has a take-out window—just like a little window at a hot-dog stand!

Busy West Wing staff people can come to the take-out window to order food to go.

Right across from the take-out window is the most secret place in the whole West Wing. It's called the Situation Room. This is where the president goes when an important or dangerous situation happens somewhere in the world. If a bomb goes off without warning, or a war is about to begin, everyone meets in the Situation Room to discuss what to do.

If you stand outside the Situation Room and listen, all you hear is silence. Does that mean the Situation Room is empty? No!

The Situation Room is soundproof. You can't hear what's going on inside. But twenty-four hours a day, there are people working in there. They keep track of important news happening around the world. They're looking carefully for dangerous situations to report to the president.

A few other rooms in the West Wing are top secret, too. They have keypad locks on the doors. No one can get in without the secret code. Who knows what's going on inside? The Secret Service might know, but they aren't telling.

The Secret Service

The Secret Service is the group of men and women who protect the president, the vice president, and their families. Wherever the president goes, Secret Service agents go, too. They surround the White House day and night—and even answer questions for people taking tours!

But being part of the Secret Service doesn't mean agents are allowed to go upstairs to the president's private rooms. One Secret Service agent worked in the White House for twelve years—and had not yet been allowed on the second floor!

The indoor swimming pool that FDR built is in the west terrace that leads to the West Wing. But in 1969, President Nixon decided to cover it over and use the space for something else. Now the pool is buried under the floor of the Press Briefing Room. Sometimes reporters go down a secret stairway and sign their names on the old pool walls.

In the Press Briefing Room, reporters and photographers gather every day to find out news about the president and the government. The president's press secretary stands in front at a podium and answers questions. Sometimes, the president himself comes in to talk.

On the opposite side of the White House from the West Wing is the East Wing. Like the West Wing, it's slightly hidden from view. The East Wing is where most visitors enter the White House. There's a large security station with bomb-sniffing dogs! Then some steps lead up to the White House itself. The First Lady's offices are in the East Wing, too. So is the White House movie theater!

Deep in the basement of the East Wing, there's a bomb shelter. It was built during FDR's time, to protect the president in an emergency. President George W. Bush was not at the White House on September 11, 2001, but Vice President Dick Cheney was there. He went to the bomb shelter after the terrorist attacks.

What's the best thing about the West Wing? Most presidents will say that they love it because it's so close to the White House—they can walk to work!

CHAPTER 6
Children and Pets

Dozens of presidents' children have lived in the White House over the years. For many of them, it was a wonderful place to grow up.

What did children love about the White House? For one thing, it's so big!

The hallway upstairs on the second floor is wide enough to be an indoor playground. These days, there are sofas, books, and a piano in the hallway. It feels like a comfy family room. But in the past, the presidents' children sometimes rode bikes or roller-skated there on rainy days.

Of course, the best place to go roller-skating in the White House would be in the biggest room—right? Jimmy Carter's daughter, Amy, thought so. She roller-skated in the gigantic East Room, which was often empty. After that, the East Room needed a new floor!

The movie theater in the White House is a great spot for children's parties. So is the bowling alley! Amy Carter and President Bill Clinton's daughter, Chelsea, both liked to bring their friends there. Everyone had to take turns, though. There's only one lane!

After the indoor swimming pool was covered over to make the Press Briefing Room, President Gerald Ford had an outdoor pool built in 1975. It became a great place for First Families to hang out. President Ford even let his dogs swim in the pool. His son Jack took scuba-diving lessons there.

When President Lincoln was alive, there was no movie theater, swimming pool, or bowling alley. So his young sons had to find other kinds of fun. Tad loved to drive a little cart, pulled by two goats, around the White House lawn. He once brought the goats into the East Room and hooked them up to pull a kitchen chair! Like Amy Carter's skating, that probably didn't do the floor much good. But President Lincoln just laughed when he heard about it.

Theodore Roosevelt's children had lots of pets. They had a baby bear, a badger, a macaw, a parrot, sheep, dogs, cats, guinea pigs, rats, snakes, goats, and more. Too many to count! His eldest daughter, Alice, liked snakes. She had a green snake named Emily Spinach. Alice took it to parties in her purse!

Alice's brother Quentin liked snakes, too. One time, he spilled a box of snakes all over a table during a meeting his father was having. Another time, Quentin brought a pony into the White House. He even took it upstairs to his brother's bedroom in the elevator!

Which children had the most pets in the White House? It's hard to say for sure. The Roosevelt children probably had the most. But President John F. Kennedy's two children, Caroline and John, might have come in second. They had nineteen pets altogether!

The Kennedys lived in the White House from January 1961 to November 1963. Caroline had a pony named Macaroni who was allowed to roam around the White House grounds. She also had pet hamsters, a gray cat named Tom Kitten, and a canary.

In 1961 Caroline received an amazing gift. The Soviet leader Nikita Khrushchev sent her a puppy named Pushinka. The puppy's mother, Strelka, was a very famous dog in Russia—Strelka had orbited the earth in a space capsule! When Pushinka mated with Caroline's Welsh terrier, she had four puppies! They named the puppies Butterfly, White Tips, Blackie, and Streaker.

In recent years, President Barack Obama's dogs have been enormously popular. Obama promised his daughters, Malia and Sasha, that they could get a puppy after he ran for election, whether he won or not. Their first dog, Bo, was so cute that everyone fell in love with him. Bo is a Portuguese water dog. He has been pictured on the Obamas' White House Christmas card at least three times. In 2013, the Obamas got a second dog, named Sunny, so Bo could have a friend!

CHAPTER 7
Time to Party!

Over the years, the White House has been the setting for all kinds of parties, big and small.

The biggest and fanciest kind of party is called a state dinner. The dinner is held in the State Dining Room, in honor of the head of a foreign country, including kings or queens. Everyone wears formal, fancy clothes—tuxedos for the men and ball gowns for the women. The White House chefs try to come up with the most delicious meals they can imagine. At one state dinner, the chef served a version of Beef Wellington, which is beef wrapped in puff pastry. But instead of beef, he used buffalo meat and called it Bison Wellington!

The tables are always set with the most beautiful china at these dinners. Every president is allowed to have a brand-new set of fine china made.

At state dinners, every plate has a handwritten menu resting on it, in beautiful handwriting called calligraphy. Guests are allowed to take their menus home as a souvenir.

Elegant state dinners don't happen very often. Most White House parties are a little bit more fun and relaxed. Bill and Hillary Clinton had their high-school reunions in the White House.

They had lots of birthday parties, too. For one surprise party, Hillary came home to find the whole house dark. Then she was led to her room and handed a wig and a costume. She had to dress up like Dolley Madison. It was a surprise party for Hillary's birthday! All the other guests were in costumes, too.

For holidays, the White House can be turned into a magical wonderland. The Christmas decorations make every room in the White House glow. There are Christmas trees in nearly every room on the State Floor. Live music plays in the Entrance Hall.

Each year, the chefs build a gingerbread house. In 2013, the gingerbread White House weighed about three hundred pounds!

In December, there's a party almost every single night.

There weren't always Christmas trees in the White House, though. Why? In early American times, people didn't celebrate Christmas that way. The first White House Christmas tree was put up for Benjamin Harrison in 1889. Teddy Roosevelt, however, didn't believe in cutting down trees. He refused to allow Christmas trees in the house. He did throw a huge Christmas party for five hundred children, though!

Other holidays are special at the White House, too. Recently, some presidents have celebrated Hanukkah with a White House party.

In the spring, the White House grounds are open to the public for the annual Easter Egg Roll. Children come and use big spoons to roll their Easter eggs down the lawn. In recent years, every child who attends the egg roll gets a souvenir wooden egg to take home. The eggs have the president's signature on them.

For Halloween in 2009, the Obamas threw a huge Halloween party. They turned the White House into a spooky house, with orange lights! Musicians were dressed like skeletons. A dancer in a butterfly costume appeared inside a huge bubble on the White House lawn!

President Obama stood at the front door and gave out treats to thousands of trick-or-treaters that year. Inside the White House, the real actors who played characters from the *Star Wars* movie roamed around for a private party. A magic show was held in the East Room. The State Dining Room was turned into a Mad Hatter's party from *Alice in Wonderland*!

Weddings at the White House

Only one president was married in the White House—Grover Cleveland. He was a bachelor when he was elected, but he fell in love with the young daughter of a friend. He and his bride, Frances Folsom, had a small private wedding in the Blue Room in 1886. Only twenty-eight people were invited. When they had a baby seven years later, she was the first and only child of a president ever to be born in the White House.

Seventeen weddings have been held in the White House. Nine of them were weddings for children of presidents. The biggest wedding was probably Alice Roosevelt's. Almost a thousand people were invited!

President Richard Nixon's daughter Tricia held her wedding in the White House Rose Garden in 1971. Her wedding dress had its own seat on an airplane when it was brought to her. Her wedding cake was more than six feet tall! The ceremony was broadcast live on TV. One of the guests at the wedding was Alice Roosevelt Longworth, who had been married in the White House sixty-five years earlier.

With parties, concerts, weddings, and other events, the White House is always busy. Sometimes there are three or four different parties on the same day! The White House serves food to as many as two thousand guests each month—and more during the holidays.

But who makes all that happen? Who cooks the food, sets up the tables, arranges the flowers, and then cleans up the mess after all those people have tramped through?

CHAPTER 8
Who Runs the White House?

It takes nearly a hundred people to keep the White House running every day. And that's not even counting the Secret Service! The staff includes chefs, butlers, maids, florists, carpenters, plumbers, painters, and more. The person in charge of that big White House staff is called the chief usher.

Usually, chief ushers keep their jobs for many years. There have only been nine chief ushers since the White House was built! One man, named Irwin "Ike" Hoover, worked there for forty-two years, twenty-five as the chief usher. He served under ten presidents. President Obama hired the first woman chief usher. Her name is Angella Reid. Before coming to the White House, she ran a fancy hotel in Arlington, Virginia, called the Ritz-Carlton!

People think the president is lucky to have so many servants taking care of his house. But guess what? The president has to pay for the First Family's food, their parties, and dry cleaning, too. Many presidents are surprised and a little bit upset when they get the first monthly bill. President Reagan's wife Nancy said, "Nobody ever told us the president and his wife are charged for every meal!"

But taxpayers pay for most of the White House staff. The president also gets an allowance from Congress for fixing up the house. In recent years, the amount has been a hundred thousand dollars! After all, with so many visitors, the place needs a new paint job every once in a while.

The White House belongs to the people of the United States, and it is a treasure. It's constantly changing, but at the same time, its history is preserved for generations to come. Thanks to all the hardworking people who take care of it every day, the White House will be here for many more presidents—and many visitors—to enjoy for years and years.

Visit the White House

For many years, the White House was open to the public twice a year—on New Year's Day and the Fourth of July. The New Year's Day tradition went on for more than a hundred years. But when Herbert Hoover was president, more than six thousand people showed up to shake his hand one New Year's Day! His hands were so swollen, he soon put an end to the tradition.

Today, if you want to tour the White House, you have to get permission through your member of Congress. Tours are open to the public several days a week.

Another annual event that's open to the public is the Easter Egg Roll. Tickets are free, but so many people want them that the White House holds a lottery. You can find out more about how to visit at the White House website: www.whitehouse.gov.

If you visit the White House, be sure to notice the words carved into the mantel in the State Dining Room. The words are taken from a letter John Adams wrote to his wife, Abigail, the day after he moved in. It says, "I pray Heaven to bestow the best of Blessings on this House and all that shall hereafter inhabit it. May none but honest and wise Men ever rule under this roof."

Timeline of the White House

1790	Congress votes to build a new capital city on the Potomac River
1792	James Hoban wins the contest to design the new "Presidential Palace"
	George Washington marks the spot where the White House will stand
1799	President Washington dies before he can ever live in the White House
1800	John Adams moves into the White House, the first president to live there
1814	British troops burn the White House during the War of 1812
1861	Mary Lincoln spends more than $20,000 redecorating the White House
1863	President Lincoln signs the Emancipation Proclamation on January 1 the White House
1865	President Lincoln is shot and his body is brought to the White House for public viewing
1877	First telephone installed in the White House
1891	Electricity is added to the White House under Benjamin Harrison's presidency
1901	Theodore Roosevelt makes "White House" the official name
1902	The West Wing office is built for Theodore Roosevelt
1933	Franklin Delano Roosevelt has the West Wing offices enlarged
1948	Harry Truman moves out of the White House so that a huge renovation can take place
	The White House is gutted and improved. A balcony is added, called the Truman Balcony
1962	First Lady Jackie Kennedy redecorates the White House and gives a tour to the public on TV

Timeline of the World

Congress adds the Bill of Rights to the Constitution	**1787**
The United States issues its first patent to William Pollard for a machine that spins cotton	**1790**
France regains Louisiana from Spain	**1800**
President Thomas Jefferson acquires the Louisiana Purchase from France for 15 million dollars	**1803**
Francis Scott Key writes "Star Spangled Banner"	**1814**
Gold is discovered in California, spurring the Gold Rush	**1849**
The US Civil War begins	**1861**
The first paper money is issued in the United States	**1862**
General Robert E. Lee, commander of southern troops, surrenders, ending the US Civil War	**1865**
Prospectors discover gold in the Black Hills of South Dakota	**1875**
Ellis Island opens as a US immigration depot	**1890**
The first motion picture theater opens in Los Angeles, California	**1902**
The Empire State Building is completed	**1931**
Jackie Robinson plays first base for the Brooklyn Dodgers, ending segregation in the Major League	**1947**
At the Lincoln Memorial, Martin Luther King gives his "I Have a Dream" speech	**1963**
MTV airs its first set of music videos	**1981**
On September 11, the North and South Towers of the World Trade Center in New York are attacked and destroyed	**2001**

Bibliography

Clinton, Hillary Rodham. *An Invitation to the White House.*
New York: Simon & Schuster, 2000.

Grove, Noel. *Inside the White House.* Washington, DC: National
Geographic, 2013.

Seale, William. *The White House: The History of an American
Idea.* Washington, DC: White House Historical Association,
1992.

White House Historical Association. *The White House: An Historic
Guide.* Washington, DC: White House Historical Association,
2011.